Say "Sorry" and heal: Finding peace through apology

Donna J. Ramos

Copyright

Introduction

Welcome to 'Say Sorry and Heal: Finding Peace Through Apology' by Donna J. Ramos – a compassionate guide to the transformative power of apologies in restoring harmony and inner serenity. Allow me to share a brief story that encapsulates the essence of this journey. Picture a moment of tension between two old friends, their bond strained by misunderstandings and hurtful words. In a courageous act, one of them offers a sincere apology, breaking the barrier of resentment and opening the door to forgiveness. Join Donna J. Ramos as she delves into such poignant narratives and illuminates the path to forgiveness, offering practical wisdom, heartfelt anecdotes, and empowering strategies to navigate the complexities of human relationships. Prepare to embark on a journey of self-discovery and healing, where every apology becomes a stepping stone toward profound peace and emotional well-being.

About the Author

Donna J. Ramos Is an acclaimed author, speaker, and relationship coach dedicated to helping individuals navigate the complexities of human connection and find healing through forgiveness. With a background in psychology and counseling, Donnal brings a wealth of knowledge and expertise to his work, drawing on years of experience in supporting others on their journey to emotional well-being. She is known for his compassionate approach and ability to offer practical insights that resonate deeply with readers and audiences alike. Through his writing and speaking engagements, Donna empowers individuals to embrace vulnerability, cultivate empathy, and transform their relationships through the power of apology and forgiveness.

Chapter 1

Understanding a non-apologizer

Once upon a time in a bustling city, there lived a man named Max, known for his larger-than-life personality and charismatic presence. Max seemed to have it all – a successful career, a loving family, and a wide circle of friends. However, there was one thing missing: the ability to apologize.

Max prided himself on his confidence and assertiveness, but this often translated into stubbornness and an unwillingness to admit fault. His refusal to apologize, even in the face of obvious mistakes, became a topic of gossip among his friends and colleagues.

One day, during a heated argument with his best friend Lucy, Max crossed a line, saying hurtful words that left Lucy feeling betrayed and wounded. Despite realizing his mistake, Max couldn't bring himself to apologize. Instead, he brushed off the incident, hoping it would blow over.

But Lucy wasn't one to let things slide. She took to social media to share her experience, sparking a wave of comments and discussions about the importance of apologies and accountability in relationships. People from all walks of life weighed in, sharing their own stories of forgiveness and healing, and offering advice to Max on how to make amends.

As the comments poured in, Max found himself reflecting on his behavior and the impact it had on those around him. With newfound humility, he reached out to Lucy and offered a heartfelt apology, acknowledging his mistake and expressing his desire to make things right.

The response was overwhelming. Lucy forgave Max, and their friendship grew stronger than ever. Inspired by his journey, others began to reassess their own approach to apologies, realizing that saying sorry isn't a sign of weakness, but rather a powerful act of courage and compassion.

And so, Max's story became a rallying cry for accountability and forgiveness, reminding us all that it's never too late to say sorry and heal.

Are they just stubborn? Or is there a commodity in their psychology that stops them from being suitable to take responsibility for their conduct and simply say they are sorry?

In any case, what might be said about individuals who can never concede they've stumbled, regardless of the situation?

What makes them unequipped for saying 'sorry' in any event, when they're clearly off base?

For these individuals, conceding bad behavior and it is excessively mentally taking steps to offer a statement of regret. Offering a statement of regret suggests that they've hurt someone else here and there, which can evoke sensations of disgrace.

Individuals who can't apologize frequently have such profound sensations of low self-esteem that their delicate inner selves can't assimilate the blow of conceding they were off-base. So their safeguard systems kick in — on occasion, unwittingly — and they might externalize any fault and even question fundamental realities to avoid the danger of bringing down themselves by offering a statement of regret. At the point when they twofold down on their unsoundness by accusing conditions, denying current realities, or going after the other individual or individuals included, non-apologizers can cause themselves to feel engaged instead of lessened.

Sadly, a large number of us erroneously decipher these individuals' delicacy driven preventiveness as an indication of mental strength. That is on the grounds that ostensibly they give off an impression of being intense people who will not withdraw. However, they don't do this since they're solid — this is on the grounds that they're frail.

Mentally talking, conceding that we're off-base is sincerely awkward and excruciating to our healthy identity. To assume liability and apologize, our confidence should be sufficient as far as we're concerned to ingest that distress. To be sure, assuming our confidence is higher and stable, we can endure the impermanent ding that such a confirmation includes — without the walls around our self image disintegrating.

The mix-up we frequently make when confronted with somebody who's routinely unequipped for saying 'sorry' is to become furious (for good explanation, obviously) and attempt to win our contention with them (since we're correct!). Yet, the miserable and baffling the truth is we can always lose. Regardless of whether we exhibited that they were off-base in obvious, inarguable realities, they will either deny those inarguable realities or turn to an individual assault by expressing something like "For what reason do you generally make things troublesome and unpleasant?!?".

Everything we can manage is to come to our meaningful conclusions as serenely and as convincingly as we can and afterward separate from the contention when it becomes ineffective — like when they question current realities, think of absurd reasons or turn to negligible comments. When they quiet down and when they never again feel went after, we can then search for indications of penitence. Might it be said that they are additional sort or kind to us? This is their approach to unwittingly attempting to retouch the relationship with us in manners that aren't threatening to their identity. By exceeding all expectations in the repercussions of their error, they can feel better about themselves as opposed to awful.

Alright, so what could you at any point do about the non-apologizers in your own life? Particularly assuming they're your relatives, collaborators or companions? Indeed, in the event that they are not individuals you connect with consistently, you can consider limiting contact with them. Yet, in the event that they are close associations, you can attempt to come to terms with them.

The most effective way to do this is to acknowledge their way of behaving — irritating for all intents and purposes — and acknowledge they're just mentally unequipped for saying 'sorry' Additionally, they won't change. Rehearsing acknowledgment can assist you separate from contentions with them and assist you with restricting your sensations of disappointment, outrage and hurt.

Then, at that point, if the non-apologizer is a nearby association of yours, you can likewise take advantage of your sympathy and empathy. Advise yourself that underneath their difficult as-a-bull outside, they are unbelievably powerless.

The primary concern is this: We as a whole have minutes when we will not concede we're off-base. In any case, when somebody never assumes liability and is routinely unequipped for saying 'sorry' a sign they're an individual with a delicate self image and a frail identity

Let's explore why some people can't say those two words: "I'm sorry." Conceding when we've accomplished something wrong is troublesome. Notwithstanding, when this hesitance to offer to set things right transforms into through and through refusal, it's an issue. The following are five motivations behind why certain individuals battle with saying 'sorry'

- They need to safeguard their self image

If somebody has any desire to safeguard their inner self, it doesn't generally mean they have areas of strength for an of pride. In some cases, conceding bad behavior might set off the delicate piece of their self image, appearing as though it's an assault on their mental self portrait. Safeguarding this mental self view takes need over nearly everything in the circumstance, prompting a hesitance to apologize and a propensity to divert fault.

- They experience difficulty perusing expressive gestures

In the event that you've at any point had a companion who doesn't appear to get when they've accomplished something wrong, they might experience difficulty perusing expressive gestures. Regardless of whether you absolutely let them know they need to apologize, they could battle to comprehend the reason why it's fundamental.

Not at all like somebody who needs to safeguard their self image, individuals who don't major areas of strength for have abilities don't necessarily have the attention to apologize when fundamental, even in the clearest of circumstances.

In any case, this can demonstrate that somebody is battling with a bigger issue. In the event that the setting is correct and you feel it's fitting, assist them with understanding the reason why conceding they put you in a terrible mood or stumbled in a discussion — yet additionally know that it's not your obligation to show somebody how to impart socially, particularly when they are off-base.

- They need the ability to appreciate people at their core

Going a stage outside not ability to grasp expressive gestures, certain individuals might need the capacity to understand people at their core (EI). Psychological wellness America characterizes EI as "the capacity to oversee both your own feelings and grasp the feelings of individuals around you."

At the point when somebody has nearly nothing or positively no EI, they battle to perceive the effect of their activities on others — not to mention relate to the feelings of those they've harmed. This blend makes it challenging for them to really apologize for the issues or agony they've caused

- They're uncertain or embarrassed about something

It's notable that insight is critical to social setting, however everything to somebody can't apologize. Regardless of whether the individual they've harmed 100% merits a conciliatory sentiment, they might fear seeming powerless or unreliable — notwithstanding legitimately realizing this isn't the standard result of saying 'sorry' Conceding they committed an error likewise puts their defects out in the open, permitting others to scrutinize how they've dealt with a circumstance.

- They're anxious about counter

At the point when an individual can't apologize, it doesn't generally mean they're doing so malevolently. They could fear reprisal or another adverse result, so rather than trying to say sorry, they attempt to stay away from it no matter what. While it's normal to need to keep away from a conflict, particularly with individuals you care about, it's not right to abstain from saying 'sorry' or to fault another person in light of nerves

What they say instead

At the point when somebody can't apologize, what they decide to say likely isn't ameliorating and won't assist with making what is going on any better. As a matter of fact, staying away from an expression of remorse and it isn't useful to embed another assertion. The following are a couple go-to phrases you could hear from somebody attempting to concede bad behavior

- "I'll say sorry when you do."

A contingent conciliatory sentiment is one of the most terrible ways of attempting and offer to set things right. It makes a stalemate where the wrongdoer and the violated individual hang tight for the other to apologize first, which just draws out an opportunity at goal. Genuine statements of regret are fundamentally unrelated of the other individual's activities — not a method for removing the consideration from themselves

- You began it."

In spite of the fact that it seems like an explanation from a contention between two children, redirecting liability is a typical assertion from anybody matured five to 85. It propagates a pattern of blame shifting as opposed to resolving the genuine issue.

- Please accept my apologies in the event that I expressed something to annoy you."

This statement of regret recognizes the possible offense however doesn't address the effect of what occurred. Saying "if" rather than giving a substantial illustration of the bad behavior makes vulnerability, suggesting an absence of mindfulness about the circumstance, or the individual saying 'sorry' isn't viewing the discussion in a serious way.

- Sorry," With a Hint of Mockery

Besides the fact that mockery subverts the genuineness and legitimacy of an expression of remorse. Assuming the individual's tone recommends craftiness, it shows the individual they aren't deserving of compromise. Much more terrible, it could raise the contention assuming that it incenses the hurt individual further.

- I'm a particularly horrendous individual, and you should n't stand me."

Certain individuals who experience difficulty saying 'sorry' may endeavor to legitimize the activity by accusing themselves and their defects. While it's feasible to feel this sort of expression of remorse, making an individual assault against their own personality generally doesn't get the responsibility or pity they anticipate.

Nonetheless, by the day's end, being wounded by a dear companion or cherished one and not getting a conciliatory sentiment is disappointing, befuddling and terrible — selfishness or not. We as a whole have times when it's challenging to apologize, however it's vital for approach struggle with a receptive outlook and feel open to conceding when you've accomplished something wrong.

Chapter 2

"I'm sorry" the magic word

Making and tolerating conciliatory sentiments nimbly are demonstrations of politeness and development, and they are significant for issues both of all shapes and sizes. Genuine statements of regret can stop unstable circumstances; it's difficult for a great many people to stay irate with somebody who gets a sense of ownership with his own decisions. "Please accept my apologies" is likewise one of the easiest and frequently most thoughtful ways of communicating compassion or lament. An employment cutback, a sickness, a demise in the family, or the passing of a pet are times when you could say sorry. At these times, keep it straightforward — you don't have to expand on the off chance that you don't know what else to say

"I'm sorry" is extremely short yet has the capacity of quieting a seething tempest. These are strong words that can save what is going on, yet tragically many individuals find them challenging to use now and again. It's possible you are hauling who is on the right track or wrong and accordingly track down the utilization of "Please accept my apologies" so challenging to say to save yourself from superfluous pressure. We are people with "*egos," albeit this characteristic is more normal in certain men. A few ladies likewise practice their self image in certain circumstances, yet not many men with my reasonable educational experience up until this point.

I recall the time I did my marriage course. This is a course which means couples take preceding their wedding festivities in the chapel. It's normally a six months course in my ward where the planning couples are being figured on the better lifestyle choice as husband and spouse in marriage. Envision two individuals meeting up from various family foundations to live on one rooftop as couples, there must certainly be conflict in for sure so the utilization of "Please accept my apologies was one of the delicate subjects that was taken care of for a solid relationship.

I'm the sort of person that esteems my tranquility of mind,it's an extravagance to me. The utilization of this word "Please accept my apologies" has never been an issue for me in any capacity since I turned into a grown-up. I figure out how strong this word can be, an enchanted word can save a nearly breaking relationship. It's an enchanted word equipped for lightening somebody's high incense on you. Luckily It's not weighty in that frame of mind to use at each required time however it is for some that I know and trust me, it doesn't necessarily in all cases end pretty well when you neglect to say "sorry" when you expected to do so .

As per the subject portrayal in this book, I have a place with the classifications of individuals who find it simple to say sorry whether I'm off-base or right. I have never wound up in a position where I found it hard to apologize, however I have been in a few positions where I was sorry in any event, when I shouldn't have done as such, yet I accomplished for harmony purpose. I have different life pragmatic cases like such however grant me to impart only one experience to you!

Sitting on my couch riding the web, I got a call from my significant other:

Hubby: Darling, how is it with you?

Me: I'm great and you?

Hubby: I'm great also; generously tidy up the visitor room, my companion Engr Imprint will be in the house in under 60 minutes, I recently completed the process of talking with him. Additionally, plan semovita with bitter leaf soup in the cooler and serve him for lunch, I will before long be home to go along with you all.

Me: Which Engr Imprint? You have never referenced that we are anticipating a guest. Is it that abrupt? Didn't your companion illuminate you before now? Why has it been illuminating me recently? Like genuinely?

Hubby: I assumed I let you know yesterday

Me: You didn't

Hubby: Simply do what I said!

Me: Speechless

Gee., Might you at any point envision the discussion above? As a person, I felt terrible! I was denied my regard as the lady of the house when I realized that a guest was coming to my home. Clearly, it skirted his brain to illuminate me since he generally does, however the least I anticipated from him is simply to say "Please accept my apologies" yet he neglected to do as such. Indeed, I'm grieved assuming he will peruse this blog...but I just wanted to share this most likely somebody could gain from my experience.

Engr Imprint who proposed to go through a night after the fact wound up burning through multi week in my home. When he at long last left, I faced my hubby over his mentality on his powerlessness to acknowledge his error by basically saying "Please accept my apologies" and prepare to have your mind blown. He began acting cold on me for a few days... maybe I don't reserve the privilege to defy an off-base demonstration? Haha

I actually returned to him, bowed down and apologized for him so I can partake in my true serenity like this and that was the finish of the case..it turned into a neglected issue till date.
This equivalent short word "sorry"made an old buddy of mine nearly lose her marriage. I beseeched her to say that unfortunately she felt so proud to apologize to her better half for her wrong doing, not even that she was basically right on the money. It took the supplication of such countless older folks to reestablish her practically broken marriage. Today, she has 3 kids with her significant other and she continued valuing me for causing her to comprehend the significance of saying sorry...she can now say sorry very quickly when required and I couldn't resist the opportunity to grin at the new turn of events.

All in all, "I'm sorry " is an enchanted word that can be pondered emphatically. It eliminates nothing from us to say sorry whether you are off-base or right. Use it however much you can and make all the difference for you

Chapter 3

Avoiding Apology pitfalls

A great expression of apology comes from the heart. In connections, we frequently wind up harming individuals, without our insight or expectation. In any case, the aggravation caused for others by us can't have a reason. A conciliatory sentiment can recuperate its vast majority. A decent expression of remorse helps in resuscitating the relationship back to its great wellbeing too. At the point when we apologize, we really want to guarantee that we ought to assume complete ownership for the offense and the aggravation brought about by us. Rather than tracking down provisos to make sense of our conduct in support of ourselves, we ought to focus on the wrongs we have done.
A good apology needs to recognize the offense straightforwardly and the aggravation that was caused.

Not many individuals appreciate giving expressions of remorse. It's difficult to concede you've committed an error, particularly on the off chance that you're in an influential position. It very well may be a catastrophe for the self image and a test to your pride, and when you're in control, you should have the responses, correct? Recognizing those errors while assuming proprietorship shows liability and development as a pioneer. Statements of regret permit us to fabricate more grounded, more dependable associations with everyone around us. They additionally assist us with developing as experts and in our jobs as pioneers."

Sadly peppering an expression of remorse with excuses is normal. Rather than saying 'sorry' for making an insincere expression of remorse, take care of business the initial time by keeping away from these mistakes:
- Not owning up to your mistake
Before you start a statement of regret, ensure you truly accept you committed the error and the craving to address it comes from your heart, says Hanke. "Finding fault or attempting to legitimize your activities will decrease the force of your

conciliatory sentiment and hurt your validity," she says. "Reasons will just strengthen the sensations of dismissal, hostility, outrage, and agony."

All things being equal, own your error. Comprehend what you ought to have done any other way and focus on rolling out an improvement later on, says Hanke.

- Indiscreetly Expressing Yourself

Before you begin to design your expression of remorse, consider what the misstep meant for the individual, says Hanke. "How would you believe they should feel after you make your conciliatory sentiment, and what are the subsequent stages to take to modify or develop the relationship?" she inquires. "When you spread out those responses, you can think about your words and plan the message."

A conciliatory sentiment can have a few layers, as well as a component of hazard, says Hanke. "Your message should be clear and resound with the audience," she says. "We get so up to speed in the feeling behind the misstep."

A major piece of what you say ought to make sense of why you committed the error and how you will determine it. Be cautious utilizing "trust," she adds. "Saying 'I trust this cheers you up' can feel awkward and reduce the message.

- Crossing the line

As well as proceeding with caution, attempt to be just about as brief as could really be expected. "If all else fails, interruption and thoroughly consider what need to say without additional words," says Hanke. "The super opposite side is the point at which we apologize excessively. The more we say, the more we disappoint."

Apologize once; more than that and the error develops to a greater misstep since you're putting a focus on it, says Hanke.

"Keep your sentences short, clear, and forthright," she says. "The misstep has proactively been finished. Individuals are more keen on why you made it happen and what you will do about it."

- Leaving out the Points of interest

Understand what you are saying 'sorry' for before you do, and don't attempt to race through it without tending to that.

"Expand on the explanation and recognize more noteworthy possession," says Hanke. "Simply come clean. Nothing awful can at any point emerge from saying reality. There may be ramifications, however we frequently fall away from reality since we dread what occurs on the opposite side. Being willing to be awkward and tending to particulars can expand your validity in lengthy run."

- Making it ndifferent

The strategy for conciliatory sentiment is basically as significant as the actual message, so don't take cover behind a screen, says Hanke.

"Perceive when an error requires an eye to eye confirmation and don't depend on innovation to do your hard work," she says. "Look at the individual straightforwardly in the eye to make an association of trust. In the event that eye to eye connections unimaginable, get the telephone so the culpable individual hears your voice and recognizes your genuineness."

Ensure your non-verbal communication and manner of speaking mirror your truthfulness. "If not, you run the gamble that your message will not be conveyed in the manner you plan,"

At the point when you apologize, recognizing three distinct things: the activity, the effect, and the intention is significant.

That being said, regardless of whether you issue a close to consummate expression of remorse — recognizing the activity, the effect, and the purpose — there's as yet single word that can cut a statement of regret crashing down. There is single word that can make a sincere "Please accept my apologies" appear everything except.

The word to look out for when it unfortunately?

BUT"
I'm sorry I lost my temper, but...
I didn't mean to hurt your feelings, but....
I'm sorry I was late, but...
I'm wasn't trying to be rude, but...

"But"t, nullifies what you expressed only preceding it. It limits the effect of a veritable conciliatory sentiment. It's like saying, *"I realize that you were harmed, But it wasn't exactly awful. It isn't so significant."*

"But" pushes the obligation of your mix-up off you and onto some other person or thing. It quietly says, "It wasn't exactly my shortcoming. I was unable to help it. Try not to fault me."

At the point when you're forced to bear a conciliatory sentiment, this feels nullifying. Your experience feels little. What's more, your aggravation feels neglected.

So frequently, when we apologize, we think our fundamental occupation is to account for ourselves — to give an explanation and a reasoning for our activity. Furthermore, "but' is an extraordinary guide in doing this.

However, the principal motivation behind a conciliatory sentiment isn't to account for ourselves. It's to recognize the activity and the effect it had. When you give the signal "however" in an expression of remorse, your statement of regret goes downhill. Since at that point, you are done tolerating liability regarding your activities and the effect they had. Furthermore, that makes an expression of remorse so strong.

Chapter 4

Navigating Relationship Challenges by saying "I'm sorry"

There is torment in our reality. There is torment among couples who convey put in a horrible mood and can't recuperate them. I consider this frequently in my work to be a relationship guide. Something else I see is an assertion from certain individuals that goes this way, "I could do without to apologize."
Some are significantly more unequivocal with, "I absolutely never say I'm grieved." This is entirely expected for certain individuals to maintain this viewpoint. That's what many individuals trust in the event that you apologize, you are giving an indication of shortcoming. Shortcoming is something many individuals accept they need to stay away from at all expense.

Saying 'sorry' can be extreme, in any event, when you really lament committing an error or causing somebody torment.
Conceding a bad behavior for the most part is difficult — particularly while doing so implies recognizing that you hurt somebody you care about.
You need to offer to set things straight, yet you could have an uncertain outlook on how. You could likewise stress over saying some unacceptable thing and exacerbating the situation.
To make a decent expression of apology, you'll need to initially have a decent comprehension of how you veered off-track.
Regret is a critical component of successful conciliatory sentiments, yet you'll presumably find it challenging to communicate genuine lament when you don't have the foggiest idea what you lament doing.

"I'm sorry for anything that I fouled up," and comparatively conventional expressions of remorse ordinarily fall pretty level — however they can likewise prompt more struggle.

Recalling your mistake may not feel all that wonderful, particularly when you realize you hurt somebody. On the off chance that you as of now feel remorseful or disheartened in yourself, you could try and try not to consider it completely. However, keep in mind: Regardless of how terrible you feel, the other individual probably feels more awful. Neglecting to recognize their aggravation does them further treachery.

Here is an example
Your flat mate appears to be disturbed, yet you don't know for what reason they'd be frantic. Subsequent to thinking about it, you notice an enormous box in the entryway and unexpectedly recollect you vowed to assist with improving their room furniture to account for another shelf. You promptly go to their space to apologize.

"I recently started to understand I overlooked assisting you with moving your furnishings. Please accept my apologies. Work has been somewhat overpowering of late, and it totally escaped my attention. I realize you needed to finish that at the earliest opportunity. Might I at any point assist you with it at the present time?"

Not certain precisely the way that you screwed up? It works out, particularly when you don't know somebody very well. It's alright to ask how you gave offense. Simply realize that a few different ways of asking are superior to other people.

Rather than:

"Okay, how did I respond this time?"
"What's going on with you today?"
Attempt:

"I've seen our collaborations have been somewhat unique recently. Did I effectively objective that?"
"Things appear to be somewhat not quite right among us, and I might want to fix that. I'm contemplating whether I effectively goal that distance?"
Then, at that point, truly pay attention to what they need to say

I've found that I've become progressively adversely affected by "conciliatory sentiment." I'm not hypersensitive to saying 'sorry' simply the word, for the most part since I think it has lost a large portion of its significance. I particularly can't stand when a conciliatory sentiment starts with "Please accept my apologies," which is typically offered protectively and is frequently trailed by "but"

All things considered, I invest a ton of energy with couples who are frantic to refocus after an excruciating or lamentable occasion. On the off chance that they're doing fix in my office, nonetheless, I make them center around a lot of other "A" words as a component of their Expression of remorse

Perhaps you answered a genuinely weak second with analysis or recklessness. Perhaps you had significant disloyalty like an issue or a habit. Assuming you're willing to stroll through these means, you'll be that a lot nearer to refocusing.

Following these five steps can help you recover no matter how large or small the offense

1. Acknowledgement
Irrefutably the main thing you really want to do is recognize your accomplice's grievance. Recognize that it hurt. Recognize that you have some liability regarding that hurt. It's critical that you not deny your accomplice's insight. It's their experience. That doesn't be guaranteed to make you awful or wrong. For sure the

main thing that is 100% valid about their experience is that they trust it. Any real statement of regret starts with an affirmation of that reality and that your accomplice isn't insane.

2. Awareness

When you recognize your accomplice's protest, you want to verbalize a familiarity with their close to home insight. This mindfulness is likewise called sympathy. Mindfulness of their protest, yet in addition their aggravation, their annoyance, their failure. Mindfulness that if you were to imagine being in your accomplice's situation, you could feel something very similar. This is a basic step. It is outside the realm of possibilities for your accomplice to genuinely excuse on the off chance that they don't feel comprehended.

3. Action

Your statement of regret ought to incorporate a pledge to change. Some noteworthy change. You could begin with a guarantee to "invest more effort," yet to that I'd say...try harder. Focus on additional consideration and expectation with regards to your accomplice's grumbling. It's anything but a commitment of flawlessness, however of exertion and activity. You should seriously think about a solitary little change that you can make everyday or week after week instead of stressing some general character change. The key to longterm relationship achievement is the little things that put value into the relationship bank reliably after some time. At the point when the bank is full, the negative episodes don't have as much power.

4. Asking

Talking about absolution, I think you want to request it. You shouldn't say, "Will you excuse me?" However you might have to request effortlessness, another opportunity, consent to refocus. I believe it's additionally vital to recognize the distinction among "hurt" and "damage." on the grounds that your accomplice is harmed, doesn't mean you expected to hurt. You can request pardon for the "hurt" without waiting be a lowlife. I've seen many individuals stay away from expression of remorse since they didn't mean to cause torment. That is not exactly the point. The fact is that you really want to go into a condition of association with your accomplice and you might have to request help

5. Answering

This last part is for the individual getting the statement of regret. There truly are just two suitable reactions to a statement of regret, and the two of them start with "Thank you . . ." The first is: "Thank you, I acknowledge your conciliatory sentiment and I excuse you." The second is: "Thank you, your expression of remorse makes a big difference to me, I actually need time to handle what occurred." to get the relationship in the groove again, you need to settle the negotiation consciously and effortlessly. On the off chance that your accomplice appears with an insightful, valid, conciliatory sentiment, you owe it to them, and to yourself, and to the relationship to appear too. What's more, assuming you're willing to acknowledge the expression of remorse and excuse your accomplice, you should be ready to set out your grumbling and abandon it. It's just not reasonable to raise a previous aggravation on the off chance that you've consented to push ahead.

Expressions of remorse and absolution are essential parts of close connections. Saying " I'm sorry " isn't tied in with conceding who is correct or who is off-base however about recognizing when a wrong is seen and understanding inclination hurt. Endeavors to apologize mean a longing to put your accomplice and your relationship in front of yourself. Without a statement of regret, some relationship issues will rot and chance decaying into disdain.

Saying "I'm sorry " signifies something else to various individuals, and we fluctuate in what we want from our accomplices subsequent to feeling hurt or double-crossed. All in all, not all expressions of remorse are made equivalent, and it is vital to comprehend what the hurt accomplice is searching for when you make a statement of regret or look for pardoning. If not, you might wind up trapped in a cycle where you that vibe your genuine endeavors to apologize are dismissed and your accomplice feels disregarded and slighted
Embrace the force of saying 'sorry' to reconnect and restore a feeling of safety and sympathy in the relationship. It is generally difficult to say "I'm sorry" but it is a vital part to a long haul, sound relationship.

Sorry is a strong word and ought not be used cheaply
The significance of an expression of remorse is massive. You were unable to envision the amount it could intend to somebody when you genuinely apologize. Along these lines, on this note, significance of conciliatory sentiment in connections is much more prominent.

In the event that you did a serious mix-up and your accomplice loves you, when you really apologize, you can be excused as well as fortifies your relationship.
Be that as it may, on the off chance that you don't esteem the significance of a conciliatory sentiment, then you could be the sole justification for the conclusion of your friendship.
Everything revolves around getting your needs right. You need to understand..... at times saying 'sorry' in the relationship can be the main right thing.

Chapter 5

Apologizing amidst Chaos

Apologizing amidst chaos can be one of the most challenging situations to navigate. When tensions are high and emotions are running wild, offering a sincere apology can feel like trying to calm a storm. Yet, it is precisely during these tumultuous times that apologies hold the greatest potential for healing and resolution.

Consider a scenario where a disagreement erupts between two coworkers during a crucial project meeting. Tempers flare, words are exchanged, and the situation escalates into a full-blown conflict. In the midst of the chaos, one of the coworkers realizes their part in exacerbating the situation and decides to apologize.

Apologizing amidst chaos requires courage, humility, and a willingness to set aside pride for the greater good. It means acknowledging one's role in the conflict, expressing genuine remorse, and actively seeking to repair the damage done. It may not immediately quell the storm, but it lays the foundation for eventual resolution and reconciliation.

In the workplace, apologizing amidst chaos can foster a culture of accountability, trust, and mutual respect. It sends a powerful message that despite differences and disagreements, individuals are willing to take responsibility for their actions and work towards finding common ground.

Outside of the workplace, apologizing amidst chaos can strengthen personal relationships, bridging divides and fostering understanding. It reminds us that even in the midst of turmoil, the power of apology has the potential to transcend conflict and bring about healing.

In essence, apologizing amidst chaos is not about extinguishing the flames of discord, but rather about planting the seeds of reconciliation and peace. It is a courageous act that holds the promise of brighter days ahead, even in the midst of life's storms.

In addition to the courage and humility required to apologize amidst chaos, it's important to emphasize the role of active listening and empathy. Truly understanding the perspective and feelings of the other party can pave the way for a more meaningful apology and facilitate a
smoother resolution to the conflict.

Moreover, it's essential to recognize that apologizing amidst chaos is not a one-time event but an ongoing process. It may require follow-up conversations, continued efforts to rebuild trust, and a commitment to addressing underlying issues that contributed to the conflict.

Lastly, it's worth highlighting the transformative power of apologies amidst chaos. While the immediate aftermath of conflict may feel chaotic and overwhelming, genuine apologies have the potential to sow the seeds of growth, resilience, and stronger relationships in the long run. By embracing the opportunity to apologize amidst chaos, individuals and teams can emerge stronger, more united, and better equipped to navigate future challenges.

Chapter 6

Dealing with defensiveness

Why do we get defensive?
Defensiveness is an oblivious approach to safeguarding ourselves against what we see as an assault. We can become guarded when we would rather not concede reality with regards to something individual. It can appear to be excessively excruciating, so we respond by dismissing input and driving it away.
Clinician Joseph Burgo, writer of the 2012 book, "For what reason Do I Do That?" says individuals frequently respond protectively when they feel accused, went after, reprimanded, or judged. [1] Our minds naturally go into "endurance mode" when they sense a danger to our security, regardless of whether that danger is only an input gathering.

Basically, we attempt to safeguard ourselves against the horrendous inclination that we might
be viewed as awkward or simply not adequate. To this end protective individuals struggle with conceding their mix-ups and managing analysis. It feels improved to keep away from the obligation, or to attempt to move the fault onto another person.

Furthermore Defensiveness can mean attempting to counter or deny reactions in regions where you feel delicate, apprehensive, liable, or underhanded. Now and again, protectiveness might emerge assuming you wanted to involve explicit adapting abilities in adolescence or immaturity to get by, and those abilities were useful at that point. As a grown-up, be that as it may, using defensiveness as an adapting expertise may never again serve you. Moreover, guarded propensities might cause hardships in driving others away or imparting.
Our cerebrums naturally kick into "survival" mode when we assume we are in a difficult situation, which might prompt overpowering feelings like displeasure or tension. Regardless of whether we aren't in actual peril, we could feel enduring an onslaught or restless when it appears as though somebody is undermining our

feeling of personality, essential qualities, or worth. This can lessen our capacity to beat cautious sentiments and make it a test to concede issue.

Rehearsing abilities like self-empathy and critical thinking could assist you with keeping quiet and delay any instinctual responses. This respite could permit you space to hear analysis, investigate why it makes you self-conscious, and make an honest effort to pursue an answer.

Defensiveness is an underhanded adversary. It hinders individual and expert development and achievement and it is an incredibly hard propensity to break. Being protective hampers your ability to understand people on a deeper level and foundationally destroys your connections, both at work and at home. It lessens your ability to be versatile and adaptable and decreases your undivided attention abilities, upsetting your capacity to settle on insightful evaluations and choices that assist you with driving all the more really.

Defensiveness is an adapting expertise — a reaction to an apparent assault or analysis. As a general rule, there are two methods for answering:

- You can deny it, act out, attack, blame someone else, or
- You can intellectually rationalize the perceived attack or criticism.

Tragically, the most well-known reaction is the first. At the point when we feel delicate, our mind naturally kicks into survival mode. A defensive individual will fault others, whether that is the individual who is carrying the grievance to them or another person. They'll reverse the situation and task onto another person ("I'm not furious; you're angry!"). Above all, they are unequipped for profoundly listening when they are in the condition of protectiveness, and they have no mindfulness of the effect. That is on the grounds that their amygdala is set off, their focal point is limited and they can't connect with their prefrontal cortex - the chief working piece of their mind. Along these lines, rather than tuning in, they for the most part assault and avoid all responsibility. Their objective is straightforward - get away from the aggravation and move.

At the time, they are not keen on change nor are they fit for utilizing interest to become familiar with the circumstance encompassing the worry or protest. All things being equal, a protective individual will utilize different procedures to endeavor to make what is happening disappear and to keep away from those troublesome sensations of not being sufficient. Their center is to explain and make sense of their insight, excuse the criticism, or finger-point. They will do everything possible to move the concentrate away from themselves

Since defensiveness is commonly subliminal, the individual doesn't know it's occurring to them, particularly not at the time. Our brain shields us from the undesirable sentiments apparently brought about by the analysis. Yet, frequently, we are not precisely deciphering what is happening. More often than not, there's no danger by any stretch of the imagination.

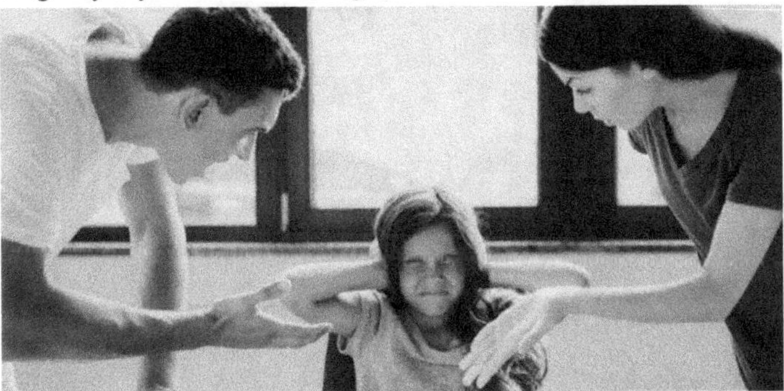

Defeating Defensiveness
Defensiveness is unquestionably difficult to defeat since a reflexive propensity gets more grounded after some time. What's more, you just have five milliseconds to prevent yourself from going down that responsive deep, dark hole. It's incredibly harming to relational connections, whether at home or at work. No change can occur until you can get through this strong guard component.

So, how can you approach someone to start to soften their defensiveness?
- Timing is everything. You would rather not approach somebody at the level of an irritated. You need to cut down the likelihood of the individual getting restless, furious or unfortunate.
- Change your tone so anything that you are drawing closer with doesn't feel like an immediate analysis but instead an idea.
- Set up the setting with the goal that the attention on can occur from here on out, as opposed to what has proactively occurred previously.

- Deal with your own reactivity, regardless of whether the individual heightens. Assuming that occurs, propose requiring a 20-second opportunity to do a few breathing activities together.
- Be delicate. Check in and ask how they are feeling all through the discussion.

Remove feeling from the discussion and move toward it as a critical thinking circumstance.

EXECUTIVE DEFENSIVENESS

Defensiveness doesn't simply occur at the lower levels in an association. I see this equivalent survival strategy uncover itself in 360 meetings with my leader training clients. A 360-degree survey depends on a representative self-evaluation and friend audits, as well as prevalent and subordinate criticism

Here are some examples of defensiveness feedback I've seen:

"He always needs to be right."
"She has to be the smartest person in the room."
"He is always quick to point fingers and blame others."
"She loves the praise. She'll always take credit for a win, but never a loss."
"He bends the truth to justify his behavior."
"I'm always walking on eggshells around her in fear that she will blow up."
"He's always focused on other teams' performances and not his own."

Defensiveness is a profound danger to somebody's confidence since they feel went after, and it's instilled to the point that individuals are in many cases totally oblivious to it. Simultaneously, most bosses are not furnished to mentally manage this degree of conduct, so by and large dealt with by a chief mentor utilizes mental conduct strategies. Doubtlessly that being cautious influences the actual individual, yet it additionally influences their immediate reports, their companions and, surprisingly, their bosses so tending to it helps the whole association.

HAVING THE TOUGH TALK

Notwithstanding, defensiveness frequently goes neglected in the working environment just on the grounds that individuals would rather not manage it. They would prefer to stay away from an awkward circumstance. Assuming this depicts you and you have somebody in your group that is cautious,

One more element to consider is whether what you are talking about is being heard accurately. You might think you are equitably clear in your conveyance, yet it very well may be judicious to remind the individual that you are not going after them, rather you are going after the circumstance to track down an answer. Keep in mind, they could have a vulnerable side and lose their capacity to listen effectively. They might be deciphering your discussion completely off-base, so asking them "What did you hear me say?" before you wrap things up to ensure everybody is in total agreement is entirely fine.

MINDMASTERY™ AT WORK

Defensiveness is a long lasting close to home propensity that is extremely difficult to change on the grounds that the individual has likely involved it as a method for getting by for as long as they can remember. A guard component is in many cases established in difficult encounters, however you can deal with it in little advances.

On the off chance that you end up being guarded, I can't imagine a superior opportunity to apply MindMastery™. In the first place, we work to recognize your temperament state when you are set off. The following stage is working on breathing activities to fix your cerebrum once again. You utilize leader working abilities to survey what is really being said versus the way that you are deciphering it and how you are feeling. Lastly, you can reevaluate your impression of being taken steps to inviting assistance to be the best chief you can be.

Rather than being shut to input, take a full breath, respite, and discover some piece of what the individual said that you accept to be valid. "Indeed, I concede that I am frequently behind schedule for work on Mondays." By recognizing a piece of the criticism with an alternate mental reaction, you are making a little move to having the option to rethink what is going on with an alternate focal point or viewpoint as opposed to becoming defensive.

Know this - you basically aren't equipped for upgrading your exhibition on the off chance that you are guarded. Truth be told, defensiveness is the very thing holding you back from rolling out sure improvement. It impedes what's feasible for you, your group and your authoritative initiative limit.

Chapter 7

Accepting Apology

It takes development and lowliness to take ownership of your errors and apologize. It likewise takes development and lowliness to acknowledge an expression of remorse after you've been violated.
Tolerating a statement of regret and pardoning somebody frequently doesn't come effectively, however there are approaches handle such circumstances with truthfulness, care and effortlessness.

One of the most significant human collaborations is the contribution and tolerating of statements of regret. Statements of regret have the ability to recuperate embarrassments and hard feelings, eliminate the longing for retribution, and create absolution with respect to the outraged gatherings. For the wrongdoer they can reduce the anxiety toward counter and ease the responsibility and disgrace that can grasp the brain with a determination and relentlessness that are difficult to overlook. The aftereffect of that expression of remorse process, preferably, is the compromise and reclamation of broken relationships."Maturely and thoughtfully tolerating a conciliatory sentiment can help you reestablish and protect your most valuable individual and expert connections

- Assuming that you get an conciliatory sentiment (apology)you can decide to acknowledge it, disregard it, or reject it. On the off chance that the expression of remorse meets the components I introduced in the past post on conciliatory sentiments, tolerating it is reasonable. Assuming you think that it is genuine, showing regret, and in the event that you feel the relationship merits keeping up with, pardoning can reinforce your bond.
- Pardoning is typically a strength. Nonetheless, in the event that the statement of regret is deficient, and you accept the oversights are conscious and manipulative, turn down the conciliatory sentiment and give the apologizer your reasons. Then, at that point, the person might attempt once more.

- Unquestionably, you ought to decline a statement of regret that needs legitimate regret. An off-gave "Please accept my apologies" is seldom satisfactory. At the point when you really do decline a conciliatory sentiment, depict what you see as lacking in the expression of remorse and check whether the other individual answers with an updated statement of regret that meets your prerequisites.
- At the point when you acknowledge a conciliatory sentiment, do so benevolently and truly with no endeavor to affront or embarrass the apologizer. Try not to take advantage of their weakness all things considered. Utilize this as a valuable chance to fortify the relationship and not as a chance to incur hurt.
- Try not to pass over an expression of remorse by saying "it's alright." Assuming you genuinely feel violated, it's not exactly alright. On the off chance that you're not prepared to acknowledge the statement of regret, or on the other hand assuming you want more from the apologizer, you must request it.
- At long last, whenever you've acknowledged somebody's expression of remorse, Continue ON. This will be therapeutic for both of you. You will actually want to surrender a portion of your hatred and start mending your injury. He/she will actually want to start relinquishing the responsibility that he/she feels for harming you. Believe that the episode won't ever repeat. Attempt to forget about it totally and center around the positive parts of your relationship.

Truly forgiving somebody who's harmed you can be all around as troublesome as getting through the torment brought about by their activities in any case. Figuring out how to thoughtfully acknowledge a statement of regret without turning over for the individual saying 'sorry' is an important fundamental ability. A very much dealt with expression of remorse can be a recuperating experience, and anybody can figure out how to deal with conciliatory sentiments with development and tact. Accepting Apology is a cycle that assumes a significant part in our connections. It expects us to explore sympathy, confidence, and taking care of oneself. Compelling correspondence and the eagerness to excuse assume a part in advancing self-awareness and close to home mending, whether it's through eye to eye corporations or innovation driven implies.

Chapter 8

Reasons why you need to apologize

What happens when your child takes a toy from another child? You ask them to apologize. What do you do when you're at the grocery store, and you accidentally bump your shopping cart into a stranger? You probably say sorry automatically

Expressions of remorse can possibly recuperate connections, mitigate put in a horrible mood, and even start to address verifiable wrongs.
Please accept my apologies." Those might be probably the least difficult but most remarkable words in the English language, with the possibly recuperate connections, alleviate put in an awful mood and even start to right verifiable wrongs. In any case, they're not generally simple to express, or to earnestly say. A large portion of us know the sensation of a statement of regret staying in our throat, in any event, when we understand how much the individual or individuals whom we've harmed might want to hear it.
Expressions of remorse truly can be considered the super paste of life as it were. I've heard that statement previously. They truly go quite far to show worry, to show that you care about the relationship, about your desired individual, to make things right. What's more, they're not generally great, as you said in your presentation. A few conciliatory sentiments are missing a lot. However, in the event that they're given from the heart and in the event that they're truly veritable and genuine in the manner they're offered and in their aim, regardless of whether the words are noticeably flawed, they can go far to showing the individual that you care about them, and that you need to offer to set things straight and fix the relationship to what it was before the mischief was finished.

Thus hence, statements of regret are perhaps of the most integral asset that individuals can use in their lives to streamline their connections, whether it's for a little affront, or joke that was unexpectedly hurtful, or for something truly major and extreme that can obliterate a relationship. Statements of regret have been known to be super strong as far as fixing the relationship, assisting individuals with refocusing, and truly being the beginning of a more extended course of compromise for a portion of those more extreme offenses. Thus in the examination that we do, we show that expressions of remorse are unquestionably powerful, particularly to the degree that they are true and seen as earnest by the person in question or the individual on the less than desirable end. What's more, that they do a ton to advance pardoning, to make recuperating in the relationship, and to lessen outrage and vengeance inspiration in the person in question.

I'm not going to apologize because I didn't do anything wrong!"

I recall my children expressing that state various times when they were youthful, and I've likewise heard it from grown-ups in the work environment a greater number of times than I want to recollect. Nobody likes to be wrongly blamed and the vast majority unquestionably don't have any desire to apologize for something they didn't do. The possibility of saying 'sorry' when we've done nothing out of sorts, or much more terrible, when we're justified, makes our blood bubble. We become angry, cautious, or attack others, none of which successfully advance the circumstance.

Be that as it may, there is an appropriate setting for saying 'sorry' regardless of whether you're not liable. It's memorable's critical that saying 'sorry' isn't a confirmation of culpability; it's an affirmation of obligation. You are getting a current sense of ownership with improving and moving past the circumstance. The following are three valid justifications to apologize regardless of whether you've nothing out of sorts:

- Picking relationship over being correct — When challenges emerge in a relationship, it's

a characteristic human sense to need to dole out fault. In the event that the other individual is off base, we can boast in the fulfillment of being correct. It's not difficult to plunge into the profound finish of the pool of affectedness. It takes close to home development to focus on the wellbeing of the relationship over the inner self taking care of should be correct. Saying 'sorry' for the aggravation and trouble of the ongoing circumstance, regardless of whether you cause it, shows you put a higher worth on the other individual than you do on the should be correct.

- Lose the fight to win the conflict — You want to have a long-range viewpoint with regards

to connections. There will be bunches of fights (e.g., contrasts of assessment, struggle, and so on) in our connections at home and work, and we'd pass on from fatigue on the off chance that we battled without holding back to substantiate ourselves directly in each case. At times it's smarter to lose the fight and apologize in any event, when you're right, for winning the greater conflict (e.g., keeping up with harmony, finishing the venture, and so on

- Take one for the group — As the pioneer, there are times you really want to take one for

the group. You may not actually have been to blame, yet on the off chance that your group has failed, you ought to assume the fault for their sake. Feeble pioneers will frequently blame everything in their group when they've committed an error. The pioneer will vindicate him/herself of any obligation and fault it in the group misbehaving. The best chiefs, in any case, apologize for the slip-ups their group make and acknowledge whatever fault comes their direction.

It's unpleasant to apologize when you've done nothing out of sorts. Each fiber of our being forces us to shout that we didn't make it happen, and to fault some other person or thing. Answering with legitimate anger frequently raises the pressure and does practically nothing to determine what is going on. On the off chance that you esteem the relationship more than being correct, will lose a little fight for winning the bigger conflict, or need to take one for you group, it's alright to apologize — regardless of whether you've nothing out of sorts

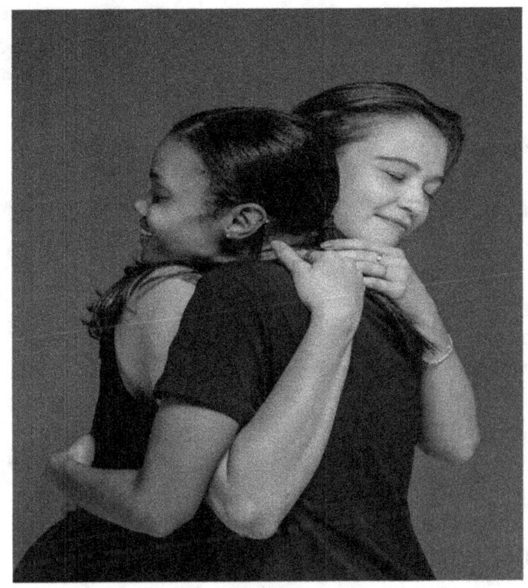

1. It Increments Mindfulness

At the point when you apologize, you find opportunity to perceive that you hurt somebody. Over the long run, this activity upgrades your understanding. You can figure out how to turn out to be more delicate or sensitive to other people. You can zero in on improving as an audience.

2. Without this mindfulness, keeping on taking part in similar dangerous patterns is simple. Statements of regret show strength-you are sufficiently able to perceive that you need to act contrastingly sometime later.

3. It Recognizes Moral Obligation

We are just human, and that implies we will commit numerous errors throughout everyday life. Definitely, you will hurt individuals, in any event, when it's unexpected.

4. To have significant connections, you should accept responsibility for your activities.

Doing so passes a readiness on to learn, develop, and accommodate your misstep.

5. It additionally exhibits lowliness to the next individual you can perceive that you have

harmed them and take responsibility for. This example might urge your friends and family to go with the same pattern.

6. It Can Assist with fixing Association

Commonly, clashes heighten in light of the fact that one or the two players need to be correct. Furthermore, our pride can disallow us from building close associations with others.

At the point when this occurs, others could feel uncomfortable around you. They may not feel as open to contradicting you since they realize it could transform into some fight.

7. The inverse is additionally obvious. At the point when you decide to take possession with

a conciliatory sentiment, you open the opportunities for social fix. Assuming somebody realizes that you are open and able to recognize your weaknesses, they will generally be bound to trust you.

All things considered, many individuals battle with the greatness of this idea. They don't apologize when it's generally significant. All things being equal, they frequently become cautious, monitored, or even confrontational.

Figuring out how to say sorry truly can have a huge effect in your connections and prosperity. We should get into a portion of the vital advantages of saying 'sorry'

Chapter 9

Discovering inner peace

Envision what is happening where you end up ensnared in a warmed contention with somebody. Feelings run high, words are traded, and you anticipate that a conciliatory sentiment should mend the injuries.

Shockingly, the individual to blame won't communicate any regret. The shortfall of an expression of remorse leaves you wrestling with a combination of outrage, hurt, and dissatisfaction.
How would you discover a sense of reconciliation in such a situation? How would you give absolution when the individual who hurt you isn't sorry?
Throughout everyday life, the quest for inward harmony and pardoning is fundamental for your close to home prosperity and self-awareness.
Forgiveness permits you to encounter serenity and concordance inside yourself. Absolution, then again, frees you from hatred and offers the chance to relinquish past damages.
Nonetheless, forgiving somebody who isn't sorry can be a difficult undertaking. It expects you to stand up to your feelings, let go of assumptions, and figure out how to recuperate without the conclusion of a statement of regret.

This section investigates the significant significance of internal harmony and absolution. It dives into Scriptural procedures for finding comfort and absolution, in any event, when a conciliatory sentiment appears to be tricky.
The advantages of absolution, as accentuated in the Holy book, are a large number. Forgiveness, first and foremost, advances inward mending and close to home prosperity. Clutching outrage, sharpness, and hatred can prompt profound and actual medical problems.
By forgiving, you discharge the weight of gloomy feelings and experience individual flexibility.
Besides, absolution encourages compromise and rebuilding in connections.

It makes the way for compromise and offers the chance for development and reestablished association.

Moreover, absolution mirrors God's personality and adjusts us to His lessons. It permits you to copy His elegance and leniency, mirroring His adoration and pardoning toward you.

Eventually, forgiveness prepares for individual change, harmony, and a more profound comprehension of God's affection.

- Diminish pressure and nervousness - forgiveness can safeguard against pressure and the cost it takes on your wellbeing.
- Shield you from sadness - Permitting yourself to pardon others can assist with safeguarding you from despondency.
- Quiet your displeasure - Unforgiveness is frequently connected with outrage, which can adversely affect your pulse, circulatory strain and safe framework.
- Expand life - Some exploration proposes that individuals who can excuse might live longer.
- Further develop heart wellbeing - Pardoning has been show to affect bringing down circulatory strain, cholesterol and the gamble of cardiovascular failure.
- Further develop rest -forgiveness is connected to further developed rest quality, which has numerous medical advantages.

One misinterpretation about pardoning is that it's an indication of shortcoming, or that it implies you're letting the individual who hurt you free. Absolution isn't equivalent to equity. There's no need to focus on being a superior individual. Furthermore, it's something other than continuing on.

At the point when you excuse somebody, you go with the decision to surrender your pessimistic sentiments regardless of whether the individual merits it. You remember that the offense happened nor do you excuse it. You don't have to make up with the individual who caused you hurt either (e.g., casualties of misuse shouldn't need to accommodate with their victimizer!)

All things considered, you settle on a cognizant choice to deliver your gloomy sensations of antagonism, disdain and vengeance — and supplant them with positive ones like sympathy, understanding and compassion. The demonstration that hurt you could continuously accompany you, yet pardoning can assist with decreasing its hold on you.

It's not just about excusing others. Perhaps you want to pardon yourself for something. On the off chance that we feel unforgiven, it can unleash devastation on our prosperity as well.

How would you figure out how to excuse? To start with, don't sit tight for a conciliatory sentiment from the individual who violated you. Here and there a reaction won't at any point be conceivable. Likewise, know that pardoning is a troublesome cycle that requires some investment and difficult work.

__The following are a couple of tips to assist with putting you on a way to forgiveness;__

- Take a stab at journaling, contemplation or supplication. Consider the actual occasion, how you responded, and how you felt. Compose a letter to the individual who violated you — you don't have to send it however communicating your sentiments can assist you with relinquishing the hurt and dissatisfaction.
- Come at the situation from the other individual's perspective. At the point when you can see the guilty party as an injured individual who isn't prepared to do more, it might assist you with supplanting sensations of outrage with sympathy.
- Discuss it with another person who you trust. On the off chance that you want some assistance, an expert specialist or care group can assist you with making progress toward forgiveness.
- Attempt unwinding or stress the board methods like profound breathing or yoga to quiet your brain.

At the point when you set forth the energy, you can figure out how to pardon. Furthermore, when you figure out how to forgive, you may then discover a sense of peace

We can all connect with having been violated by somebody. We might have the option to pardon a relative, companion or accomplice for a minor slight fairly without any problem. It very well may be significantly more hard to relinquish a significant bad behavior. You could figure the other individual doesn't merit it, however YOU do.

Unforgiveness can jeopardize your wellbeing. Consistently holding onto pessimistic sentiments keeps you worried and restless. You get so enveloped with past wrongs that you can't partake in the present. Individuals who cling to hard feelings are bound to encounter various medical problems.

The demonstration of forgiveness then again, can be a useful asset to your prosperity.

Chapter 10

Learn Apologizing Rightfully and Respectfully

However much I endeavor to be caring, there are days when I crash and burn. I'll awaken feeling terrible, the children will be cantankerous, and 1,000,000 seemingly insignificant details won't turn out well for me. My chemicals will be unsound, the financial plan won't adjust, and I'll get some horrible news. Life will burden me - it happens to us all.

While I'm feeling not exactly lovely, I'm bound to commit errors. I become upset. I make statements that are heartless. It's frequently unexpected, yet in any case, I hurt others.

Whether it's my companion, my partner, my mate, my kids, or even an outsider - nobody should be dealt with cruelly on the grounds that I am having a terrible day. So I should gain proficiency with an example in retroactive thoughtfulness - to figure out how to apologize really.

It's never something simple to do. Conceding you were off-base and taking ownership of your horrendous acts is a lowering encounter. A genuine statement of regret leaves you defenseless and uncovered and very awkward. Be that as it may, it likewise leaves you with a superior comprehension of yourself as well as other people, and ideally will give you the sympathy to stay away from a similar terrible way later on.

Connections can be awesome supports against pressure, however relationship clashes can likewise cause extensive close to home agony and stress. Knowing how to apologize — and when — can fix harm in a relationship, yet in the event that you don't have the foggiest idea how to apologize truly, you can really make things worse.A earnest and compelling conciliatory sentiment is one that imparts certified sympathy, regret, and lament as well as a guarantee to gain from your mix-ups. At the end of the day, you want to truly accept you accomplished something wrong and feel frustrated about the hurt you caused. Here are simple tasks to assist you with figuring out how to apologize earnestly and successfully.

Pick Your Strategy

Verbal statements of regret are proper under most conditions, however setting things right recorded as a hard copy can likewise have its advantages. Many individuals experience uneasiness with an eye to eye statement of regret, and keeping in mind that this distress alone is definitely not a valid justification for a composed conciliatory sentiment, it very well may be a component — particularly assuming your inconvenience influences your capacity to articulate your thoughts.

Working out your statement of regret in a letter, email, or even text can give you an opportunity to mindfully create your conciliatory sentiment, trying to acknowledge liability, express regret, and reaffirm limits.

Then again, composed statements of regret might be excessively formal for certain errors and not private enough for other people. Furthermore, on the off chance that the composed statement of regret isn't trailed by a reaction, you might be left with an unsettled struggle.

Keep your statement of regret straightforward and direct. Assuming that you get out of hand, you'll make it about yourself rather than the individual you violated. This can disdain and dissolve trust.

A genuine conciliatory sentiment can likewise bring help, especially in the event that you have responsibility over your activities. A statement of regret alone doesn't eradicate the hurt or make it alright, however it lays out that you know your activities or words were off-base and that you will endeavor harder in the future to keep it from recurring.

Not saying 'sorry' when you are off-base can be harming to your own and proficient connections. It can likewise prompt rumination, outrage, disdain, and aggression that may possibly develop over time.Knowing when to apologize is essentially as significant as knowing how to apologize. By and large, you suspect that something you did — deliberately or coincidentally — caused another person bad sentiments, it's smart to apologize and clear the air.While an earnest statement of regret can go quite far toward repairing a relationship, individuals are frequently reluctant or incapable to make this stride. Conceding you were off-base can be troublesome and humble.

1. Name what you fouled up. Try not to simply say: "Please accept my apologies you got injured." That is not taking ownership of your activities. Rather say: "Please accept my apologies I called you guileless" or "Please accept my apologies I pushed past you." Be explicit about your activities and why you are saying 'sorry' for your way of behaving.

Significantly more critically, don't extend your activities as another person's shortcoming. "Please accept my apologies you made me act that way" isn't an expression of remorse by any stretch of the imagination. Nobody can cause you to respond in a specific way. You are the one liable for your activities and words.

2. Use compassion. Perhaps your activities could never have harmed you, yet the truth of the matter is that they hurt another person. Recognize their sentiments as authentic. Attempt to see things their way, and let them in on you grasp their hurt. For instance: "Please accept my apologies. I appeared for supper so late. I realize it caused you to feel irrelevant, and I ought to have regarded your time more."

Normally individuals get injured on the grounds that you are putting yourself first, so ensure you come at the situation from their perspective while you're saying 'sorry'

3. Make everything about you. In the event that a battle has ejected, and you're quick to approach and concede you were off-base, keep the conciliatory sentiment about you. Try not to zero in on what the other individual fouled up or how they incited your activities. Bringing up the other individual's

deficiencies and requesting a proportional statement of regret will sabotage all the other things you say. Assuming you're just saying sorry so they will say sorry as well, you want to reevaluate your purposes behind saying 'sorry' in any case.

4. Keep clarifications brief. You ought to contemplate the root reason that you were harsh before you apologize. Like I said previously, nobody can cause you to respond in a specific way, so anything the other individual did is superfluous. Perhaps you were having a shaky outlook on yourself or perhaps you were under a ton of stress at work or perhaps you were feeling a piece desire.

You can account for yourself assuming the explanation is important, however keep it brief and recollect that it doesn't legitimize your way of behaving - and say as much. "I was worried about my venture cutoff time, however that doesn't make it acceptable for me to shout at you. Please accept my apologies. I acted that way."

5. Let it go. Whenever you've apologized, now is the ideal time to follow Frozen and let it go. What occurs next isn't doing you. As hard as it might be to put yourself out there and really apologize, the truth of the matter is nobody owes you their pardoning. Not something can be procured. Pardoning is a gift, and truth be told, one you won't ever merit.

Try not to attempt to compel somebody to acknowledge your statement of regret. If the other individual would rather not fix the relationship, regard their choice. Relinquish any disdain and outrage, and indeed, attempt to see things their way. You can indeed do a limited amount a lot of before now is the ideal time to let it go.

Offer to set things straight

In the event that there's anything you can do to correct the circumstance, make it happen. It means a lot to know how to apologize with earnestness, and a piece of that genuineness is an eagerness to act.

The Primary concern

Certified expressions of remorse are generally difficult, however that can be a significant piece of patching or keeping up with significant connections. With compassion, an open heart, and a portion of fortitude, you can make the strides you want to make an earnest and legitimate statement of regret.

Conclusion

In wrapping up 'Say Sorry and Heal: Finding Peace Through Apology' by Donna J. Ramos, we've traversed an enlightening path towards personal growth and relational harmony. Through meticulous exploration and insightful discourse, Ramos has shed light on the profound significance of apology in our lives.

As we draw the curtains on this insightful journey, let us carry forward the pearls of wisdom gleaned from these pages. Ramos reminds us that apologies are not merely linguistic gestures but transformative catalysts that have the power to mend fractured relationships and foster emotional well-being.
With each turn of the page, Ramos invites us to embrace the noble art of apology with reverence and sincerity. Let us heed her call to action, armed with newfound insights and a renewed commitment to fostering empathy and understanding in our interactions with others.
In parting, 'Say Sorry and Heal' stand as a beacon of inspiration, guiding us towards a future marked by mutual respect, compassion, and authentic connection. As we bid adieu to this literary voyage, let us carry forward its profound teachings and continue to nurture a world where apologies are not just spoken, but lived.

Acknowledgement

I extend my deepest gratitude to God Almighty
Furthermore , i would like to express my sincere appreciation to my family for their unwavering support and encouragement throughout this journey. Your love and understanding have been my rock during the highs and lows of the writing process.
I am also grateful to the readers who have embraced the ideas presented in this book and allowed them to resonate in their lives.Last but not least, I extend my heartfelt thanks to all those who strive to make the world a better place through the power of apology and forgiveness. Your efforts inspire me every day.This book is dedicated to each and every one of you. Thank you for being a part of this journey.